All About
COLOR

Elizabeth Rusch & Elizabeth Goss

Charlesbridge

What do you know about color?

Color doesn't exist.
The sky is not blue.

The grass is not green.
A violet is not even violet.

When there is no light,
there is no color . . .

because color is light sending messages
to your brain.

Color can tell you when to stop
and when to go.

Color can be a warning . . .

or a call for help.

Color can help you stand out . . .

or blend in.

Color can even remind you
who is on your side.

Color can make you see red . . .

or feel blue.

Color can even brighten your day.

You can use color . . .

to color your whole life!

MORE ABOUT COLOR

Color is created through the interplay of three things: light, the materials in an object, and you.

Light is made up of waves of energy. When light hits the surface of an object, some of the waves are soaked up (absorbed), and some bounce off (reflect). The waves that bounce off hit your eyes, and your brain recognizes them as different colors.

The surprising thing is that colors are not constant. The color of something can change depending on the light that shines on it. Think about how different someone's face looks in bright sunlight, at sunset, next to a computer screen, or in the glow of a fire. Notice how the changing lights of your day affect the colors around you.

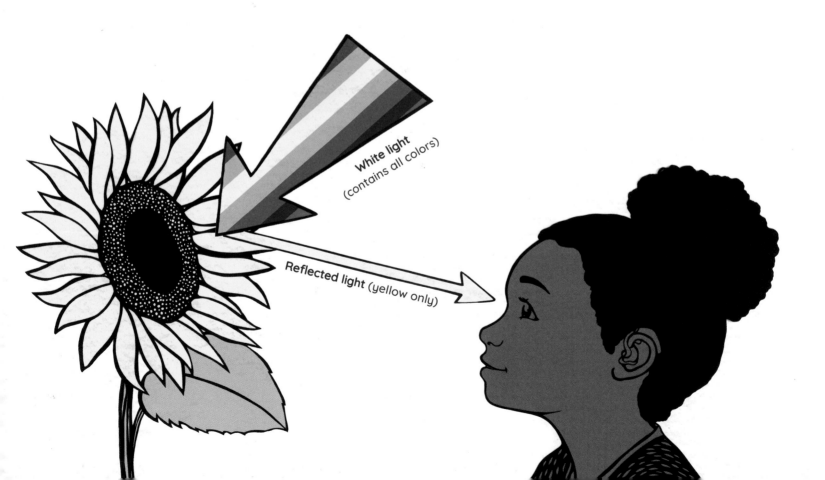

White light
(contains all colors)

Reflected light (yellow only)

Color can also change if the surface changes. As a penny ages, its color can change from bright copper to brown, black, or green. A leaf may seem to shimmer bright white when it gets wet. The same color can even look different depending on what colors are nearby. Notice how the orange square seems to change color depending on the surrounding color.

The colors you see are personal to you. The way your brain reads waves of energy may be quite different from how someone else's brain interprets them! Most people can see one million or more colors. But about one in every twelve people have difficulty seeing red and green. Do you see a number in the circles to the bottom right? If not, you may have colorblindness.

Colors help us identify things, understand our world, and make decisions. How does color affect what you wear, what you eat, and how you feel?

A good way to understand color and emotion is to think about your favorite color. How does it make you feel? Also consider your favorite piece of clothing, favorite crayon, or favorite place. How does color affect your preferences?

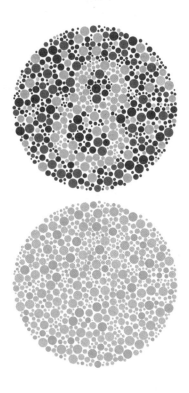

Artists revel in color! They use it to create mood and show what is important in a picture. How can you use color to draw attention to something—or hide it? How might the same picture feel different if you colored it with just blue colors or just yellow colors? What colors might make your art look lively, sad, or even funny?

What can you say with color that you can't say any other way?

For Liz Goss, who has taught me much about color.—E. R.

For Travis, my one in vermillion. And for Liz Rusch,
who taught me all about storytelling.—E. G.

Text copyright © 2024 by Elizabeth Rusch
Illustrations copyright © 2024 by Elizabeth Goss

At the time of publication, all URLs printed in this
book were accurate and active. Charlesbridge,
the author, and the illustrator are not responsible
for the content or accessibility of any website.

Published by Charlesbridge
9 Galen Street
Watertown, MA 02472
(617) 926-0329
www.charlesbridge.com

Printed in China
(hc) 10 9 8 7 6 5 4 3 2 1

Illustrations done in cut paper
Display and text type set in Quicksand by
    Andrew Paglinawan
Printed by 1010 Printing International Limited in
    Huizhou, Guangdong, China
Production supervision by Jennifer Most Delaney
Designed by Jon Simeon

Library of Congress Cataloging-in-Publication Data
Names: Rusch, Elizabeth, author. | Goss, Elizabeth Ames,
    1987- illustrator.
Title: All about color / Elizabeth Rusch; illustrated by
    Elizabeth Goss.
Description: Watertown, MA: Charlesbridge, [2024] |
    Series: All About Noticing | Audience: Ages 4–8 |
    Audience: Grades K–1 | Summary: "This concept picture
    book explores the art, science, and emotion of color,
    encouraging young readers to see the world
    differently."—Provided by publisher.
Identifiers: LCCN 2022058024 (print) | LCCN 2022058025
    (ebook) | ISBN 9781623543532 (hardcover) | ISBN
    9781632893246 (ebook)
Subjects: LCSH: Color—Psychological aspects—Juvenile
    literature.
Classification: LCC BF789.C7 R873 2024 (print) | LCC
    BF789.C7 (ebook) | DDC 152.14/5—dc23/eng/20230530
LC record available at https://lccn.loc.gov/2022058024
LC ebook record available at https://lccn.loc.
    gov/2022058025